Designer Tips

- Do not cut patterns from book. Create re-usable templates from template plastic. Template material can usually be purchased in the quilting section of most stores. This saves time and is more durable than a paper template.
- UTEE becomes very hot when it melts, do not touch or it will burn.
- To remove unwanted texture such as fingerprints in the UTEE, simply remelt.
- Peeling off the white liner first is a great habit to get into. You will save yourself a lot of hassle if you get into this habit. If you have trouble removing the pink, simply heat it until it starts to curl.
- To increase tackiness, apply heat gun to the affected area. It is always a good idea to set all your projects with a heat gun. This increases the tackiness of the tape allowing your work to become more permanent.
- Apply a spray acrylic sealer to silver and gold projects to prevent them from tarnishing. I use clear Krylon.
- Always save scraps of tape, many projects can be made out of them, eliminating waste.
- Keep large areas of the pink liner for future use. These make great masks for future projects.
- Also to keep fingers from sticking to projects, apply the pink liner to an area you are not working on. Touch only where the pink liner is. This will keep the tape at a max for tackiness.
- Most of the tape and bead projects are very forgiving. Make sure that you have placed tape in all areas where you desire embellishment. If an area is lacking tape, simply cut a scrap and place on the unexposed area. It does not matter if there are slight creases or lumps in the tape, it will not be noticeable when the project is finished.
- I work on a piece of craft foam over a glass cutting board. I find that this really helps the beads not to bounce and provides an excellent base when I want to cut tape using my X-acto knife.

Basic Supplies: Double-sided Redliner Tape and sheets (includes Terrifically Tacky, Ultimate Bond and Wonder Tape), Seed beads, Bugle beads, Micro beads (includes No-hole beads, Tiny Marbles, Treasure Beadz, Zamora Beadz, Teenie Weenie Beadies, etc.), Wire, Ultra-fine Glitter

1. Shape wire. Apply to sticky tape.

2. Sprinkle beads on surface.

3. Wrap wire around beads on body.

4. Glue pin back to dragonfly.

Use this elegant dragonfly as a pendant or an embellishment for a greeting card.

Dragonfly Pendant
by Linda Peterson

MATERIALS: Gold *Artistic Wire* (20 and 24 gauge) • Redliner double-stick tape • Micro beads (Silver, Gold) • Assorted Amber beads • Silver 7 mm bead • Pin Back • *Omni Stick* glue • *Krylon* sealer

INSTRUCTIONS: Shape a 4" piece of 20 gauge Gold wire into wing shape beginning with coil. Repeat. Remove white liner and place each shape onto flat tape. Replace liner (shiny side down) and cut out. Remove white liner. Place chosen bead on upper wing. Sprinkle this half with Silver beads. Sprinkle the bottom with Gold beads. Repeat this on opposite wing.

Antennae: Bend a 4" piece of wire in half and coil each end. Wrap 24 gauge wire around bend, leaving approximately 6" extending. Squeeze with pliers. String Silver bead onto thin wire until it meets antennae. String on remaining Amber beads of choice. When finished, wrap the wire around the beads going up toward the head. Sew one wing onto body and wrap end wire around bead to secure; repeat with other wing. Use Quick Grab glue to affix the pin back to the dragonfly. Spray project with sealer to prevent tarnishing of Gold and Silver beads.

**Wing Pattern
Make 2
Reverse 1**

Bold, graphic and fun!

Black/Silver Pendant & Earrings

by Linda Peterson

MATERIALS: Redliner double-stick tape • Black Cardstock • *Artistic Wire* (20 gauge Black; 22 and 24 gauge Silver) • Bamboo Skewer • *UTEE* (Platinum, Black) • Black Micro beads • Black bugle bead mix • Assorted Black beads • 36 " of Black jewelry cording

TIPS: These designs can be created using a variety of color schemes. To save time in future projects, coil the wire around the entire length of bamboo skewer and cut off desired amount leaving the rest pre-made for future projects. In this project, we are making one pendant set at a time. If you are making a variety of pendants in various color schemes, sandwich your cardstock between two sheets of tape. Use a stylus to impress the pattern into the red liner and cut out several shapes all at once.

PENDANT INSTRUCTIONS: Coil Black wire around bamboo skewer. Cut a $1^1/2$" long coil. Cut out pendant pattern. Sandwich between two pieces of tape. Trim edges of tape next to pattern. Peel off one side of liner, set aside. Cut two $3^1/2$ inch pieces of black wire. Beginning at point, outline shape leaving $1^1/2$" extending out the top of the pendant. Repeat for other side. Trim corners to point if necessary. Bend wires as shown in diagram. Using the red liner as a mask, replace the liner as shown in diagram and sprinkle Silver UTEE onto tape. Remove mask and sprinkle on tiny Black beads and bugle beads as desired. Finish by sprinkling entire Black area with Black UTEE. Peel off back liner bend wire coils forming a slight loop big enough for the coil to fit into. Press coils to back side of pendant. Sprinkle entire back with Black UTEE. Use pliers to hold and heat set UTEE. Let cool completely before touching. Embellish with a 4" piece of Silver wire. Coil one end. Start at back and wrap around front to desired design. Glue into place. Thread a 4" Silver wire thru the coil. Add beads and loop ends to finish. Thread jewelry cord thru the loop and back up. Hold with pliers and wrap Black wire around to secure in place. Trim cording flush with wire. Repeat for other side.

EARRINGS: Cut out basic shapes. Outlining of earrings is done with UTEE instead of wire. Embellish earrings as above. Create two jump rings by cutting two pieces of Silver wire $1/2$" and bending until edges meet. Poke hole in center of top and insert Silver jump ring. Coil wire as previously shown, create zigzag by using pliers and bending the wire back and forth. Finish with a bead. Loop and bring wire to back, trim to desired length. Attach jump ring to bottom of coil. Earring size can be adjusted by changing the size of the coil and the amount of the zigzags.

Earring Wire Pattern

Pendant Pattern

Earring Pattern Make 2

Pendant Diagram

Beaded Beauties

Note: Dots on patterns indicate where to bend wire with pliers.

Large Leaf Wire Pattern

Medium Leaf Wire Pattern

Earring Leaf Wire Pattern Make 2

Easy, fashionable and fun!

The colors of Autumn are truly beautiful! This elegant artzy leaf design can be used as a pendant or an embellishment for a greeting card.

Artzy Leaf Choker Set
by Linda Peterson

MATERIALS: Olive Green cardstock • Redliner double-stick tape • *Artistic Wire* (Brown 22 gauge, Gold 26 gauge) • *UTEE* (Bronze, Gold) • Gold metallic Micro beads • Assorted beads • Choker hoop • Fish hook earrings

INSTRUCTIONS: For choker, refer to Leaf Card on page 19 for Basic Leaf Construction. Make 3 leaves using the patterns on this page. When making decorative coil, create loop to hang leaf on choker. Thread assorted beads on Gold 26 gauge wire and wrap around choker. Place leaf pendants on choker and thread wire through loop to secure in place. For earrings create 2 leaves using the patterns on this page and the Basic Leaf Construction technique on page 19. Attach leaves to fish hook earrings.

Rose Applique Frame

MATERIALS: Ready-made White frame • Tissue paper in flower color of choice and leaf color • Redliner double-stick tape • 20 gauge *Artistic Wire* to match flowers and leaves • Clear *UTEE* • Glitters

INSTRUCTIONS: Apply tissue papers to tape. Create whimsical flower shape using pattern. Press wire shapes to tape (with tissue paper already applied). Cut out. Sprinkle with clear UTEE and glitters. Heat set. Repeat the same steps for the leaves. Glue these appliques to frame where desired. Curl wires to create tendrils and attach to frame.

Rose Applique Frame Pattern

Leaf Applique Frame Pattern

- *Quick & Easy!*
- *Inexpensive!*
- *Fun for teens!*
- *Use your favorite colors!*

Beaded Frames

by Linda Peterson

Wild n Whimsical Frame Back Pattern

← **Cut out opening in Frame Front only.** →

Wild n Whimsical Frame

MATERIALS: Purple cardstock • 2 sheets Redliner double-stick tape • Blue & Silver micro beads • Blue/Purple bugle bead mix • Purple ultra-fine glitter • Purple large flake glitter • 18 gauge purple *Artistic Wire* • *Yasutomo* Purple Mizuhiki paper cord • Purple tissue paper • Hot Glue • Clear *UTEE* • X-acto knife

INSTRUCTIONS: For this project, I find it easier to work off the spool and it also eliminates waste. Although wire can be used around the window, I use paper cording because it is much easier to manipulate. Trace the pattern onto template material, cut out. Trace pattern onto cardstock. Use a stylus to mark the window of the frame. Tape one side. Cut out window with X-acto knife. Remove adhesive liner. Outline top and bottom of frame with purple wire leaving 1/4" extending off edges on each end. Beginning 4" from end of wire, outline sides leaving 4" extending on each side top and bottom. Curl wires as

shown. Bend loops in top wires to go around side wires. Outline window with paper cording. Bead as desired. Sprinkle on glitters, small silver beads and finish with clear UTEE. Heat set.

BACKING: Cut tape using pattern. Press tissue paper to both sides. Outline three sides with strips of tape. Set aside.

LEGS: Working off the spool and using pattern as guide, loop top of wire. Slide fingers down 3" and bend at a 90-degree angle. Curl around to create coil, following the pattern as guide. Clip when finished. Repeat for another leg. Place flower shape onto tape. Cut around. Apply clear UTEE and glitter to one side and purple cardstock to other. On back of frame, mark leg positions with pencil, making sure frame stands uniform. Lay loop over marking and hot glue. Peel off pink liner from backing and place on frame back so that the opening is at the top.

Wild N Whimsical Frame Front Pattern

TIP: For variety, enlarge or reduce patterns on a copy machine. For a fun grouping, use other bead colors to match your décor. Just remember to use the corresponding color of cardstock. For fun, add purchased wire words such as PRINCESS, etc… glue to frame at desired location.

1. Cut out cardstock and cover with adhesive tape.

2. Cut out window with X-acto knife. Remove liner.

Flower Power Frame

MATERIALS: Redliner double-stick sheets • Light Blue tissue paper • Micro bead mixes (Blue/Green, Silver) • Aqua bugle bead mix • *Yasutomo* Mizuhiki Paper cording (Light Blue, Green) • 18 & 22 gauge Kelly Green *Artistic Wire* • Miniature silver bucket • Floral styrofoam • Stylus • Hot glue

MAKING THE STAND: Turn bucket over onto tape, trace and cut out circle the size of the opening. Fill bucket with styrofoam to the brim. Place tape over top. Outline with green paper cording. Cover entire top with Blue/Green mix beads. Cut a strip of tape ½" wide, bead with Aqua bugle bead mix. Wrap around outside of bucket.

FLOWER FRAME: Cut two flower shapes from tape and press tissue paper to one tape shape. Use stylus to mark window opening on this tape shape. Carefully cut out window area with X-acto knife. (I cut out on craft foam mat over glass cutting board.)

Remove red liner, outline the outer edge and window area with the blue paper cording. Bead as desired with Aqua bugle mix. Place tissue paper on both sides of remaining shape. Cover with tape and press tissue paper over this to give a finished look. Hot glue edge leaving open between dots on pattern. Match backing and place over glue. Press firmly. Trim edges with scissors.

HANGER: Cut a 2" piece of cording, loop and add to top back of flower.

STEM: Bend 24" piece of Green wire in half. Bend fold down 1" and then back up ½". Wrap the stem with the same color of Green wire.

With 22 gauge Green wire, shape leaf shapes using pattern, leaving a 4" wire extension on one side of the leaf. Place onto tape. Cut out and bead both sides. Wrap extension wire around stem. Press stem into center of bucket base and hot glue into place. Hang flower frame from top of stem.

3. Outline window with paper cording or wire.

4. Sprinkle beads on frame.

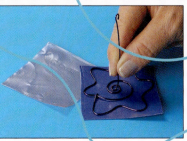

5. Place flower shape on taped cardstock.

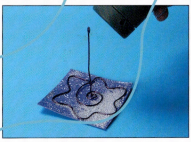

6. Place UTEE on flower shape and heat set.

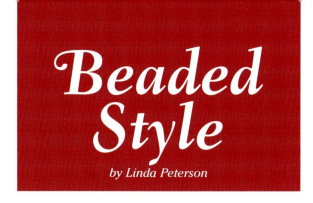

Beaded Style

by Linda Peterson

This candle is designed to complement the poinsettia project. However, it is a great project for any occasion, especially weddings!

Poinsettia Candleholder

MATERIALS: Micro beads (Kelly Green, Metallic Red) • Green & Gold bugle bead mix • Three 5mm gold beads • Red tissue paper • 2 Redliner double-stick sheets • Red glitter • *Artistic Wire* (20 & 22 gauge Kelly Green; 20 gauge Red; 22 & 26 gauge Gold) • 1/8" Aluminum *Amaco* Armature Wire • Green floral tape • Six 10mm amethyst colored beads • *Yasutomo* Mizuhiki paper cording (Greens & Golds) • Candlestick

POINSETTIA FLOWER SHAPES: Cut ten 7" pieces of Red wire. Use pattern to create shape. Use pliers to achieve nice bends. Leave excess wire extension. Each poinsettia contains ten petals. Peel white liner from flat sheet, apply tissue paper. Peel off red liner. Apply wire petal shapes and replace red liner. Press down firmly, making sure all the tape comes in contact with the wire. Cut out around wire edges. Remove liner and sprinkle bugle bead mix onto bottom portion of petal. Dip remaining area into Metallic Red beads. Trim off excess tape around edges if needed. Repeat until all petals have been beaded. Wrap ends with floral tape. Loop wire through Gold beads and twist to secure. Repeat for three stamens. Wrap all three stamens together with floral tape. Add a 6" piece of 22 gauge Green wire to stamens and wrap with floral tape.

ASSEMBLY: Wrap one petal at a time around stamen, secure with floral tape until you have wrapped 5 petals on the top row. Repeat this step in a second row just below top row.

LEAVES: Using instructions above, create leaf shapes with 20 gauge Green wire. Bead as above using Green bugle mix and Kelly Green beads. Wrap end with floral tape. Secure to Poinsettia with floral tape.

CANDLEHOLDER: Wrap 22 gauge Gold wire around an 18" piece of Silver armature wire. Make loop at one end and coil around candlestick two times. Continue to coil, creating a big base. Attach poinsettia to base by wrapping the extending wire around the candleholder. Use Gold wire to secure into place if needed.

ACCENTS: Cut Mizuhiki cords to 6" in length. Wrap one end with floral tape. Attach a 4" piece of 22 gauge green wire to the same end of cords and secure with floral tape. Wrap wire end around stem of flower to secure Mizuhiki where desired. Create berries by wiring them the same as the stamens. Wrap ends together with floral tape adding an extension wire if necessary. Wrap wire into place on arrangement. Shape arrangement as desired.

TIP: If necessary, secure the arrangement to the base with 26 gauge Gold wire.

Simple Embellished Candlestick

MATERIALS: Candlestick • Redliner double-stick tape • Gold beads • Pearl Ex powder (interference gold) • Big soft bristled brush

INSTRUCTIONS: Wrap tape around entire candle. Sprinkle beads lightly onto candle to desired coverage. When finished dust entire candle with Pearl Ex powder to remove unwanted tackiness.

Poinsettia Petal Pattern Make 10

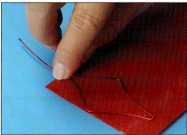

1. Lay petal-shaped wire on adhesive sheet.

2. Sprinkle bugle bead mix on lower half.

3. Apply micro beads on remainder.

4. Wrap 5 petals around stamen. Repeat for second row of 5 petals.

Beauty and style are the results you'll get with instant roses. They are so easy to make that you will have time to not only make your bouquets and corsages, you will be able to add those finishing touches to candles, centerpieces and chairs. An added plus, they make wonderful keepsakes.

1. Sandwich petals between two sheets of adhesive.

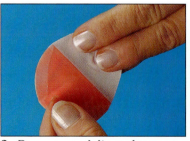

2. Remove red liner from one side of petal.

3. Remove red liner from other side of petal.

4. Dip petals into clear beads.

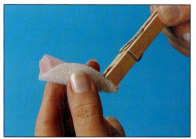

5. To create center, roll petal from one side to other.

6. Wrap next petal, covering edges of previous petal.

7. Wrap floral tape around base of rose and wire stem.

8. Embellish with ribbon and pearls.

Instant Roses

by Linda Peterson

Instant roses can be made with a variety of wire colors and bead combinations to match any decor.

Instant Glass Beaded Roses

MATERIALS: Precious Petals Pink rose petals by *Hirschberg, Inc.* • 2 sheets of Redliner double-stick tape for each rose • Clear Micro beads • 18 gauge floral wire • White floral tape for bridal projects or Green floral tape for bouquets • Clothespin

Each rose uses 6 petals; each rosebud uses 3 petals.

Rose Petal

INSTRUCTIONS: Peel the white liner from an entire sheet of tape. Place rose petals in a row down onto tape. Smooth with fingers. Peel white liner from second tape sheet. Place over rose petals to sandwich them between the tape. Cut out shapes with scissors. Remove red liner and press pointer and middle finger on the tape at the bottom center of petal. Remove red liner from opposite side. Stick thumb to underside center. Dip into clear beads. Peel off fingers and lay aside. Repeat until all the petals have been beaded.

ASSEMBLING THE ROSE:

Tip: When assembling several flowers at a time, use a clothespin to hold the centers of the rose in place while working on the others. To create the center, roll one petal from left to right, pressing tape together at the bottom. Center the next petal where the edges of the center overlap and wrap around. Repeat these steps pinching together at the bottom after each petal is applied. Curl a small loop at the top of the floral wire stem. Push the opposite end down the center of the rose until it comes out the bottom. Pull through until the wire loop is deep inside the rose. With pliers, pinch the bottom of the rose all around the wire. Wrap floral tape around base of rose and extend down onto the floral wire, adding leaves where desired. Trim to desired length.

Leaf Pattern

Champagne Flute

MATERIALS: Precious Petals Pink Rose by *Hirschberg, Inc.* • 2 sheets and scraps of Redliner double-stick tape • 5 assorted pearls • 18 gauge floral wire • White floral tape • Clear micro beads • 24" of 1 1/2" sheer White ribbon

INSTRUCTIONS: Create rose following general instructions. Bead three leaves and wrap around rose stem. Add pearl embellishments. Trim rose stem to 10 inches. Tie ribbon bow around rose stem. Coil stem around stem of goblet. There are a variety of Precious Petals available today in various colors and flower petals. Experiment!

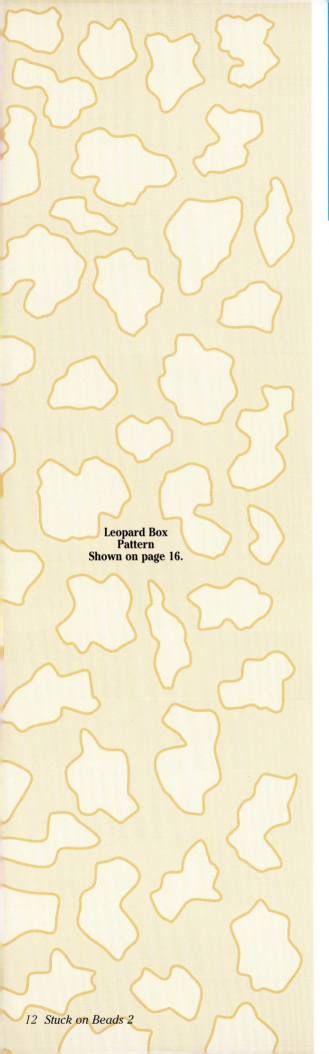

**Leopard Box
Pattern
Shown on page 16.**

Hearts and Flowers

These keepsake boxes are perfect for storing your precious mementos and special treasures.

1. Cover box with adhesive.

2. Add designs to box with plastic lacing.

3. Dip box in beads and press beads down.

4. Remove plastic lacing.

5. Sprinkle glitter over box to fill design lines.

Beaded Keepsake Boxes

by Lizette LaForge

MATERIALS: Redliner double-stick tape (One 9" x 11" sheet; one roll of 3/4" trim tape) • Micro beads (Pearl, Clear) • Heart-shaped box • *Amaco* Country Garden Paper Shapes (3-6 Leaf shapes; 6 Flower shapes) • 1 hank *Toner Plastics* Lace Nooodles • Lavender Ultra-fine glitter • *Fiskars* small scissors and craft knife • *Undu* (to remove adhesive from scissors) • Permanent marker

INSTRUCTIONS: When you place tape on surfaces, be sure to remove any air bubbles before removing the red liner. This can be done by pressing with your fingers. Place the box top on the 9" x 11" tape sheet and draw a line as indicated. Set aside the excess to be used later. Place tape sheet on the table, red liner side down, peel off the white liner and place the

closed side of the box top on the exposed tape. Turn this over and press tape firmly to box top and remove any air bubbles. Trim the tape to the edge of the box top. Remove red liner from box top. With plastic lacing, add designs to box top. Dip box top into Pearl beads, press down beads, pull off plastic lacing and set aside. Cover box bottom with 3/4" tape, beginning at center back of heart. Keep working your fingers across red liner to keep this as straight and smooth as possible. Trim any overlapping tape at center back. Before removing red liner, use craft knife to trim away any excess tape from top or bottom edges of box. Remove the red liner from the box bottom. Create designs on box bottom with plastic lacing. Dip into Pearl beads, press the beads down and remove lacing. Sprinkle Lavender glitter all over both the box top and bottom, covering thoroughly. Shake off excess glitter.

TIPS: Use a Ziploc bag and shake project with glitter in bag. Tap gently to remove excess glitter while project is still in bag.

Using the piece of tape saved from step 1, cut pieces of tape so you have enough to cover both sides of the flower and leaf shapes. Peel away white liners and cover both sides of shapes. Remove air bubbles. Trim the tape on the flower and leaf shapes, right to edge of shapes. Peel away red liner from both sides of the shapes. Place your finger on underside of a leaf shape (using finger to mask off the center).

Make sure your finger is CLEAN and dip shape into Clear beads. Press beads down firmly and peel the shape off your finger and add to the heart box top. Repeat this process for the rest of the shapes, doing leaves first, then flowers.

Let dry for 24 hours, allowing the adhesive to fully cure.

6. Shake off excess glitter in a ziploc bag.

7. Peel off white liner; position flowers in long strip.

8. Fold strip over onto the adhesive.

9. Press air bubbles out.

10. Trim around flower shapes right up to the edge.

11. Peel off red liner with finger on underside of shape.

12. Dip shape into clear beads to coat on both sides.

13. Peel shape off finger and apply to box top.

Tote Bag Fun

Take this tote on your next big adventure. The print was transferred to the bag with bonding tape and covered with no-hole beads and glitter to give the print an almost holographic effect. The giraffe's spots are fabric paint.

Giraffe Tote Bag

Giraffe Tote Bag Pattern

by Lizette LaForge

MATERIALS: Canvas tote 14" x 14" • Four sheets of Redliner double-stick tape • Giraffe print fabric (approx. 6 1/2" x 8 1/2") • *Tulip* Dimensional Light Brown Fabric Paint • Micro beads (Pearl, Clear) • Iridescent White Ultra-fine glitter • *Aleene's* Jewel-It embellishing glue • Paintbrush • Brown *Sharpie* Marker • Scissors

INSTRUCTIONS: Trace giraffe pattern onto side of bag in pencil, then with Brown marker once general shape has been placed. Only trace out the "spot areas", which will leave the white pathway between spots free of marker. Using tape sheets, cover side of bag, right over the traced out spot areas. Be careful to match up the tape edges carefully so entire surface is completely covered. When placing the tape down, remove the white release liner and place tape directly onto bag, leaving red release liner intact. Using scissor handles or a bone folder, rub tape vigorously to be sure it's well adhered to bag surface and removing any air bubbles. Peel off the red release liner from side of bag. Cover the giraffe print with Pink sticky tape, leaving the red release liner over the print. Trim off any excess tape. Carefully place the giraffe print in the center of the taped area, working slowly from one side to the other, avoiding air bubbles and wrinkles. Leave the red release liner over tape on the print at this time. Once giraffe print is placed, you may cover some of the tape areas with red liner scraps so your hand won't stick to the tape if you place it down as you paint the giraffe spots. Using Light Brown dimensional fabric paint, carefully fill in giraffe spots using paint sparingly. Use tip of bottle to add texture to spot surfaces. Continue working across the whole bag until all the giraffe spots are covered. Let paint dry. (A blow dryer may be used to accelerate drying.) Once paint is completely dry, add the Pearl beads to all remaining tape areas. Pathways between giraffe spots should still be sticky and Pearl beads will adhere to them. A simple way is to place beads into a large container and then dip bag into container. You can also place beads into a large plastic bag and then add your canvas bag, shaking vigorously until all the paths are coated. Press down beads well. Using ultra-fine Iridescent White glitter, shake carefully into Pearl beaded areas. This will help to fill in the hole areas between the beads. Shake off excess glitter. Peel off red release liner from giraffe print and bead it with Clear beads. Paint completed project with Jewel-It embellishing glue, making sure to use quick strokes over beaded areas and to be very sparing with the glue. If you have painted over an area once, do not go back over it again until it is thoroughly dry; otherwise, you may disturb the beads from the tape surface.

TIP: You may accelerate drying process with a blow dryer if you like. Bag should be vibrant and flexible. With enough glue coating, beads should withstand abrasion well. Do not wash or wet project throughout. If you must clean bag, lightly wipe off beaded surface area with a damp cloth.

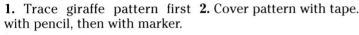

1. Trace giraffe pattern first with pencil, then with marker.

2. Cover pattern with tape.

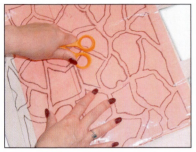

3. Rub tape firmly to ensure consistent adhering.

4. Cut the tape sheet the size of giraffe print.

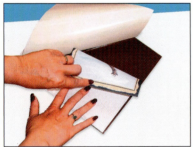

5. Remove white liner and place giraffe print face down.

6. Rub firmly to smooth out any air bubbles. Trim excess tape.

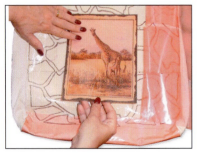

7. Place giraffe print in the center of bag.

8. Fill in the giraffe pattern with fabric paint.

9. Use blow dryer to accelerate drying time.

10. When paint is dry, fill in with no-hole beads, then glitter.

Out of Africa

by Lizette LaForge

Elephant Box

MATERIALS: Cardboard box with lid • Redliner double-stick tape • Elephant print fabric • Micro beads (Black, Clear) • Black ultra-fine glitter by • 1 hank *Toner Plastics* Lace Nooodles

INSTRUCTIONS: Apply tape to box lid and sides of box. Determine where the edge of the box lid sets and extend tape on box $1/8$" above, so that the edge of the pattern is covered by the box lid. Press tape firmly to remove any air bubbles. Cut tape sheet the size of elephant print. Remove the white liner and place elephant print face down. Rub firmly to smooth out any air bubbles. Leaving the red release liner over the print, trim off any excess tape. Peel off the red release liner from box and box lid. Carefully place the elephant print in the center of the box top, leaving the red release liner over elephant print at this time. Create designs on box and lid with plastic lacing. Dip box and lid into Black beads; press the beads down and remove lacing. Sprinkle Black glitter all over the box and lid, covering thoroughly. Shake off excess glitter.

TIP: Use a Ziploc bag and shake project with glitter in bag. Tap gently to remove excess glitter while project is still in bag.

Peel off red release liner from elephant print and bead it with Clear beads. Press beads firmly to set.

Giraffe Box

MATERIALS: Cardboard box with lid • Redliner double-stick tape • Giraffe print fabric • Black fabric (to cover box and lid) • Clear micro beads

INSTRUCTIONS: Cover box and lid with black fabric. Cut 2 pieces of Ultimate Bond tape the size of the giraffe print. Carefully sandwich giraffe print between tape sheets; rub firmly to remove any air bubbles. Remove red liner from front of giraffe and dip fabric into no-hole beads. Press beads firmly to set. Remove red liner from back of giraffe fabric and carefully center on box lid. Press firmly to attach and remove any air bubbles.

Leopard Box

MATERIALS: Cardboard box with lid • Redliner double-stick tape • Leopard print fabric • *Tulip* Light Brown Dimensional fabric paint • Micro beads (Black, Clear) • Black ultra-fine glitter • *Aleene's* Jewel-It embellishing glue • Paintbrush • Brown *Sharpie* marker

INSTRUCTIONS: Paint and bead the box and lid separately following the general painting and beading instructions for the Giraffe Tote Bag. Determine where the edge of the box lid sets and extend leopard pattern on the box $1/8$" above so that the edge of the pattern is covered by the box lid. Pattern is on page 14.

Glistening Vase

by Diane Trepanier

MATERIALS: Vase • Redliner double-stick tape • 1 package Imitation Gold Leaf • Micro beads (Gold/Silver mix, Clear) • Household bleach (gel type works best)

INSTRUCTIONS: Completely clean surface of vase. Cover the entire vase with tape, clipping any curves to make the tape fit. Patch any open spaces with small bits of tape. Working in small areas, remove sections of tape release and apply Gold leaf. After all areas are covered with Gold leaf, lightly burnish with a soft cloth. Dab on bleach over entire vase. Dry thoroughly. As the bleach dries, a verdigris patina will appear. A second coat of bleach may be applied if more patina is desired. After the vase is completely dry, cover the entire vase again with tape. Remove tape release from around the top and bottom edges. Dip edges in Gold/Silver beads mix. Working in sections, remove tape release and sprinkle a few Gold/Silver beads. Then fill in with Clear beads. Press beads into the tape. Continue with other sections until the entire vase is covered.

These cards look expensive and time consuming… but really, they are quite inexpensive and quick! As you will see in this book, there are a variety of uses for the same technique. Using the leaf pendant as inspiration for this card, you will see how easy it is to create an artzy-looking card that anyone would love to receive. Let your creativity flow by exploring a combination of different shapes. Use these projects to jump-start the flow!

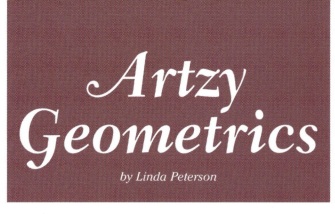

Artzy Geometrics
by Linda Peterson

Elegant and Artzy Leaf Handmade Card

MATERIALS: 5" x 7" Kraft paper card • Burgundy paper • Tree Bark paper or patterned paper of choice • Olive Green cardstock • Redliner double-stick tape sheets, 1/4" wide tape • Brown 22 ga. *Artistic Wire* • *UTEE* (Bronze, Gold) • Gold micro beads • Black/Silver bugle bead mix • Black bead • *Yasutomo* Glue-it • *Amaco* Rub N Buff • Pop Dots

INSTRUCTIONS: Glue 5" x 7" Burgundy paper onto card front. Apply glue unevenly around edges, sprinkle with bronze UTEE and heat set. Apply very small amount of Rub-N-Buff with fingers around edges. Cut out a 4" x 5³/4" piece of tree bark (coordinating) paper. Apply glue unevenly around edges, sprinkle with bronze UTEE and heat set. Adhere to front of greeting card with pop dots. Cut out a 3" x 5" piece of Olive Green cardstock. Apply 1/4" double-sided adhesive tape around edges. Dip edges into Bronze UTEE. Sprinkle tape lightly with gold UTEE and tiny gold beads. Heat set. Apply tape strips around edges on back. Peel off red liner. Center onto tree bark (coordinating) paper; press down to attach. Repeat the above steps on a 3" x 3" piece of Olive Green cardstock. Apply pop dots to all corners and one in center. Press onto card as shown.

BASIC LEAF CONSTRUCTION: Cut a 12" length of Brown wire. Place wire onto pattern; hold with pointer finger on right hand. Follow the pattern using your left pointer finger to guide it. Curve wire gently until the first dot. Remove right hand and grip pliers. Place pliers on the dot and bend. This creates a sharp bend. Continue using your index finger to guide until the next dot. Use pliers to create bend. Repeat this process until you have completed the pattern. Peel white lining back. Press wire shape to the tape surface. Replace white liner. Smooth down with fingers making sure all wire points touch tape. Cut out around pattern. Remove white liner; use it to mask half of leaf. Sprinkle exposed tape with Gold beads and Bronze UTEE. Remove white liner; sprinkle Black bugle bead mix to exposed tape. Fill in by sprinkling with Gold beads. Tap off any excess. Remove backing. Sprinkle Bronze and Gold UTEE onto backing. Heat set. Let cool. Thread on beads as desired. Finish by coiling the extra wire or trim off if desired. Trim unwanted tape or beads from leaf with scissors. Attach to card with pop dots.

VARIATION: To create a gift card, punch two small holes in the square Olive Green card. Add pin back to leaf. Add pin to leaf using holes. Apply pop dots in all four corners of Olive Green card. Press dots onto the greeting card.

Artzy Leaf and Spiral Pattern

Geometric Artzy Card

MATERIALS: 3" x 8¹/2" card • Burgundy paper • Tree Bark paper or patterned paper of choice • Olive Green cardstock • Redliner double-stick tape (sheet & 1/4" wide tape) • 22 gauge Brown *Artistic Wire* • *UTEE* (Bronze & Gold) • Gold micro beads • *Yasutomo* Glue-it • Pop Dots

INSTRUCTIONS: Following the basic instructions on the leaf card, apply Burgundy paper to card. Rub edges with uneven amounts of glue and dip into UTEE. Heat set. Cut a 3" x 7³/4" rectangle from tree bark (coordinating) paper. Edge with glue and UTEE. Apply pop dots in corners and center over Burgundy paper. Cut 3 pieces of Olive card stock. Apply same technique as the Olive cardstock on leaf card. Bend a 6³/4" piece of Brown wire into triangle shape following pattern. Bend a 5¹/2" piece of Brown wire into circle coil following pattern. Bend a 6¹/2" piece of Brown wire into square coil following pattern. Peel white backing from flat tape. Press on shapes. Reapply backing and cut out. Remove white backing, sprinkle each shape with Gold beads and UTEE. Peel red liner off back, sprinkle with UTEE and heat set both sides. Apply pop dots to back of shapes and press on Olive squares. Apply 1/4" wide tape strips to back side, press to Tree Bark (coordinating) paper.

1. Mask part of leaf shape and dip into beads.

2. Pull off mask and dip into bugle bead mix.

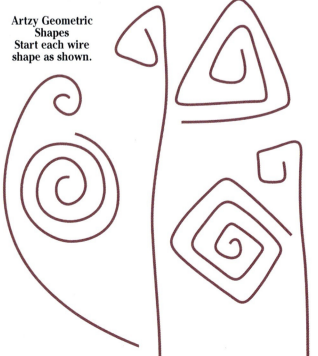

Artzy Geometric Shapes
Start each wire shape as shown.

1. Edge paper with glue.

2. Dip edge into UTEE.

3. Apply beads and UTEE to geometric shapes.

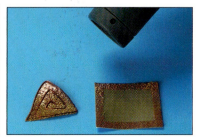

4. Heat set shapes.

Mini Purses

by Linda Peterson

Carry your credit cards and a small amount of money in these useful mini purses. You can make a purse to match every outfit!

1. Stamp designs on front and back, heat set.

2. Apply bugle bead mix.

3. Sprinkle UTEE and heat set.

4. Assemble mini purse.

**Mini Purse
Pattern
Fold and crease
along dashed lines.**

Black and Gold Purse

MATERIALS: Redliner double-stick tape • *Yasutomo* Gold Mizuhiki paper cord • *UTEE* (Black, Gold and Clear) • Black/Gold bugle bead mix • *Rub n Buff* (Gold leaf; Antique gold) • Fibers • Rubber Stamps (*Hampton Art Stamps* #2282 Face in Square; *Hero Arts* #K1952 Bamboo With Leaves) • Gold Pigment Stamp pad • Jewelry Cording • *Artistic Wire* (20 and 24 gauge Dark Blue) • Tissue Paper (Black, Brown) • *Gem-Tac* (optional) • Hot glue • Stylus • Ruler
INSTRUCTIONS: Trace pattern onto tape and cut out. Mark fold lines and crease with stylus using ruler as a guide. Remove white liner and place onto Black tissue paper. Remove red liner, leaving a $1/4$" strip of red liner over side flap as a mask. Stamp designs on front and back panel as desired and heat set slightly. Outline front of purse and purse flap with paper cording. Sprinkle bugle mix along stamped edges and onto purse flap. Sprinkle Clear UTEE over front and back panel, heat set. Place a $1/4$" strip of Redliner double-stick tape along bottom of back panel, remove red liner. Remove red lining strip, fold over front (beaded side out) and secure with tape flap. Press to secure. Cut out circle of tape the size of a quarter. Remove white liner and coil paper coil onto tape. Remove red liner. Dip into clear UTEE and heat set. Place a scrap of tape on back and attach to purse flap. String beads onto 26 gauge wire as shown, looping each end of wire with pliers to secure. Poke wires through bottom of purse. Create two Black jump rings by bending a $1/2$" piece of wire until ends meet. Poke a hole into each upper side of purse. Place a 1" piece of wire through Black bead, loop on both ends. Attach one end to jump ring. String jewelry cord through other end and then back up. Wrap with wire to secure and cut off excess cording. Coat the purse with a couple of thin layers of Gem-Tac and allow to dry between layers. This ensures the beads will remain in place and adds durability. While the purse is delicate, it can still be useful. It is great to carry identification and a bit of money.

Brown and Gold Purse

Follow basic instructions above. Use Brown tissue paper for the inside. Place a $1/4$" tape strip at the bottom of the back panel over tissue paper. Fold over to create bag. Put your hand inside and remove red liner. Sprinkle the outside edges with Gold UTEE. Sprinkle Clear over entire project. After tackiness disappears from the UTEE, lay down or hold with pliers to heat set. The UTEE will bead. Let cool. Lightly rub Gold Leaf and Antique Gold Rub n Buff over surface with fingers until you are satisfied with the finish. Stamp a piece of Black tissue paper with design. Place tape over it and sprinkle it with Clear UTEE and outline edges with Gold as desired. Heat set. Cut fibers to desired length. Knot at top. Glue to Black center. Place this over front flap as embellishment. Use same fibers for handle. Cut to desired length. Make a small knot at both ends. Lift flap. Starting in center of crease, run a bead of glue and press one end into the glue and across flap. Starting from the center again, run a bead of glue in opposite direction, press other knot into glue as before. Finish with any other beadwork you desire.

Designer Artzy Pens

by Linda Peterson

Watch out, everyone will be 'borrowing' these fancy pens! Great for gift giving! The Bic Round stick pens are great because they can withstand the heat of the embossing gun. Refill cartridges can be easily replaced with pliers.

Basic Pen

MATERIALS: *BIC* Round Stick® pens • Redliner double-stick tape • Assorted Bugle beads in various colors • Micro beads in various colors • UTEE • Assorted wires in coordinating colors to match beads • Black cardstock • Assorted Feathers (mine are pheasant feathers) • Assorted fibers in coordinating colors to match beads • Assorted jewelry findings • Basic tools and supplies

BASIC PEN INSTRUCTIONS: Cut a strip of tape slightly longer than the length of the pen from the base to the top and 1⅛" wide. Remove white liner. Place the pen along the edge and roll the tape around. If it happens to not meet exactly, cut a strip of scrap tape to fit.

White Pen

MATERIALS: Clear *UTEE* • Silver micro beads • Pearl seed beads • 24 gauge Silver *Artistic Wire* • 8mm Pearl • Silver charm

INSTRUCTIONS: Follow basic pen wrap instructions. Apply beads and UTEE randomly as desired, heat set. Cut a 16" piece of wire and begin wrapping pen, with pearl at top of pen. Attach Silver jewelry finding to the curled end of wire.

Feather Topper Pen

MATERIALS: Gold micro beads • Red, Green & Gold bugle mix • Silver wire • Silver, Bronze and Gold *UTEE* • 12 fluffy feathers (Pheasant) • 26 gauge Silver *Artistic Wire*

INSTRUCTIONS: Follow basic pen wrap instructions. Moisten your fingers slightly and rub onto feathers to calm down the fibers and make them easier to work with. Group 4 feathers together, wrapping the bottom with wire. Remove red liner ½" from top. Stick feathers to tape. Secure by wrapping more wire. Wrap top of pen with ½"strip of tape over wire. Remove red liner a little at a time. Sprinkle pen with bugle mix, micro beads and Silver, Gold and Bronze UTEE in random pattern as desired. Coil a 14" piece of Silver wire to desired length or shape. Place coil onto tape, apply UTEE and beads as desired to both sides. Heat set. Let cool. Wrap the coiled wire around the pen as desired.

Black Fiber Pen

MATERIALS: Gold & Clear *UTEE* • Gold seed beads • Black bugle mix • Black micro beads • 26 gauge Gold *Artistic Wire* • Fibers

INSTRUCTIONS: Follow basic pen wrap instructions. Hold pen by top. Expose adhesive and begin sprinkling on the Black bugle mix, leaving some areas free of beads. Follow with Black micro beads until you are satisfied that you have covered the entire pen. Press beads firmly into pen with fingers, heat set slightly. Cut a 2" square of Black cardstock. Place tape on one side, remove liner and sprinkle with Gold UTEE on edges and clear in the center. Heat set. Cut a 12" length of Gold wire. Place wire onto back side of cardstock with approximately 2" extending above. Cover with a piece of tape. Remove red liner and apply Clear UTEE to finish. Beginning with wire extension, wrap wire around pen starting at the top, going down until the wire is coiled around pen. Cut three to four pieces of fibers approximately 4" long. Tie in knot at the top. Add feather and glue this to the center of the Black cardstock.

Geometric Shape Pen

MATERIALS: Bronze & Gold *UTEE* • Gold beads • Black bugle mix • 22 gauge Brown *Artistic Wire*

INSTRUCTIONS: Follow basic pen wrap instructions. Apply beads and UTEE randomly as desired, heat set. Cut a 14" piece of brown wire, shape into triangle. Remove white liner of tape and place triangle to tape. Apply UTEE and beads as desired, heat set. Add decorative beads if desired just above shape. Coil opposite end and wrap wire around pen ending the triangle shape where desired.

Geometric Pen Pattern with Bead

Purple Pen

MATERIALS: Platinum *UTEE* • Purple/Silver micro bead mix • 22 gauge Purple *Artistic* wire • Silver charm • Miscellaneous beads

INSTRUCTIONS: Follow basic pen wrap instructions. Remove liner and sprinkle on beads and UTEE as desired, heat set. Cut a 14" piece of wire and begin wrapping, adding larger beads periodically as desired. Attach Silver charm finding to top of pen.

1. Remove white liner of tape; wrap around pen.

2. Remove red liner and sprinkle on UTEE and beads.

3. Heat set with heat gun.

4. Wrap wire around for embellishment.

1. Remove liner from petal shape, cover with beads.

2. Thread pearl bead on wire for center of flower.

3. Assemble flower petals and center.

4. Coil silver wire for base.

5. Dip base coil into UTEE, heat set.

6. Glue flower back to loop in base.

Mini Flowers
by Linda Peterson

Very quick and easy projects to make, these daisies are perfect for that last minute gift!

Placecard Flower Pattern

Daisy Flower Petal Pattern

Twist wire into leaf shape and wrap end of wire around beginning wire or stem.

Top of Holder Spiral Pattern

Base of Holder Spiral Pattern

Beaded Daisy Candle Votive

MATERIALS: Candle with votive • Redliner double-stick tape sheet • Micro beads (Pearl, Clear) • 5mm Pearl beads • Plastic lacing • Large rhinestone or flattened marble for center • Tissue paper (White, Magenta) • 22 gauge White *Amaco FunWire* • Ultra-fine transparent glitter • Pliers • 24" of 1" sheer White ribbon

HINT: Do not complete this project the day before the wedding as the Pink tissue paper will stain your hands. Wear protective gloves to prevent staining hands.

The Zip cord technique using the plastic lacing is a great way to create filigree texture on the tape.

INSTRUCTIONS: Cut a 2" x 4" strip of White tissue paper. Cut a 4" x 4" piece of Magenta tissue paper. Wet the Magenta paper with water and dab onto one long edge of the White leaving the opposite edge White. Dry with heat gun. This gives a watercolor effect.

PETALS: Cut six pieces of White wire into 3" lengths. Bend in half, giving a nice gentle loop for the petals. Repeat for 6 loops. Sandwich the White/Pink tissue paper between tape. Peel off the red liner. Place the wire petals onto the tape so that the White area is at the top of the petal. Repeat this until all petals are on tape. Replace White liner and cut around outer edge of wire with scissors. Remove both liners and dip into clear beads. Cut a circle the size of a nickel. Peel off white liner. Place the petals around in a circle. Press firmly to secure. Glue a clear glass marble to the center.

Measure the diameter of votive. Cut 1 1/4" wide strip that length. Peel off white liner and dip both edges into 5mm Pearl beads. Lay plastic lacing on in swirls in the center of the ribbon. Sprinkle on micro beads. Remove lacing to expose pattern. Sprinkle with transparent glitter. Remove pink liner and wrap around center of candle base. Hot glue daisy to front.

Beaded Floral Placecard Holder

MATERIALS: Redliner double-stick tape • 18 gauge Silver & 26 gauge White *Artistic Wire* • 24 gauge white *Amaco* FunWire • White floral tape • Pearl micro beads • One to three 5mm pearl beads • Clear *UTEE* • Hot glue

HINT: Stretch floral tape before wrapping. It will stick better.

INSTRUCTIONS: Petals: Cut six 2 1/2" pieces of white FunWire. Bend in half, giving a nice gentle loop for the petals. Repeat for 6 loops. Cut six 3" pieces of 26 gauge white wire. Bend in half, to form an inner loop for petal reinforcement and to connect petals together. Peel off white liner and press white FunWire petal shapes to the tape. Press 26 gauge inner shape with ends extending off petal. Replace white liner and cut around outer edge of wire with scissors. Twist ends together to create a petal with a stem. Repeat this 6 times. Peel off white liner and dip into Pearl micro beads. Remove red liner and dip into the Pearl micro beads.

Center: Cut three 2" pieces of 26 gauge white wire. Thread a wire through hole in large pearl bead. Bend wire in half and twist ends together. Place all three pearl beads together and twist wire to secure.

Assembling the flower: Secure each petal to the center wire stem. Pinch flower together with pliers up near the base. Wrap with 26 gauge wire around base. Trim to stem to 1/4".

Base: Working off the spool, begin coiling one end of Silver wire with pliers. Continue to coil until it is approximately the size of a nickel. Measure down 1 1/2". Create a small loop. Measure down 1 1/2". Bend in a 90-degree angle. Begin the base coil with pliers, continuing until the base is approximately 1 1/2" in diameter. Peel off white liner and press bottom of base to the tape. Cut out. Coat both sides of the tape with Clear UTEE and heat set. This provides a nice secure base for the wire to sit in. Press the stem of the flower thru the loop and secure with hot glue.

celeste

1. Tint edge of White tissue paper with Pink tissue paper.

2. Trim around wire edges of petals.

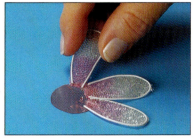

3. Place beaded petals on adhesive circle.

4. Make design on adhesive strip with plastic lacing.

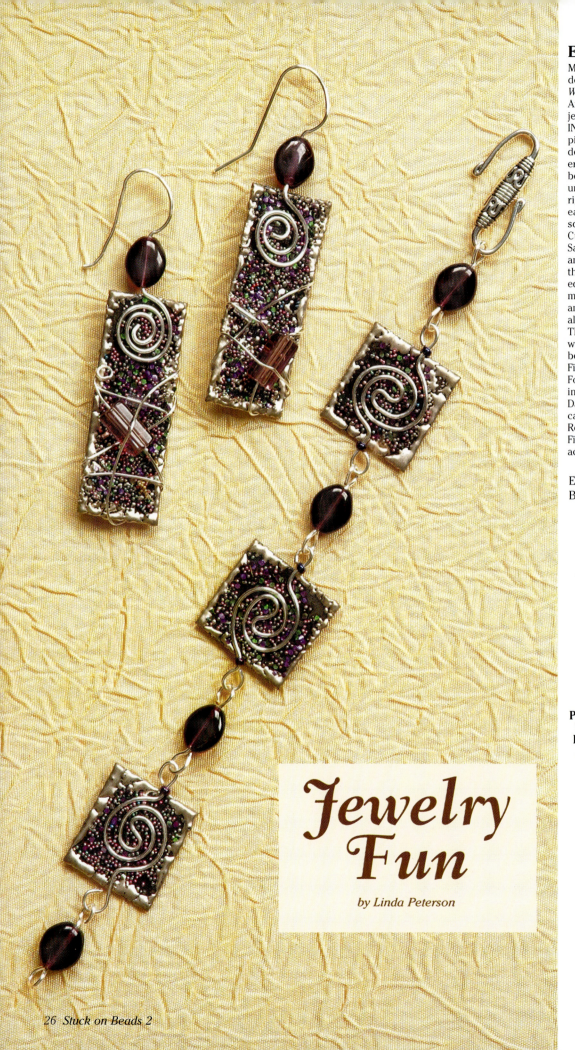

Earring and Bracelet Set

MATERIALS: Black cardstock • Redliner double-stick tape • Silver 22 gauge *Artistic Wire* • Purple micro bead mix • Assorted Amethyst Beads • Platinum *UTEE* • Clasp jewelry finding

INSTRUCTIONS: For each square, cut a 5" piece of Silver wire. Bend wire in half to determine center. Grasp center with pliers and begin curling. Once the curl has been formed, wrap ends of wires around until you have one end extending to the right and one to the left. Create a loop on each end. Repeat this for as many squares as you desire.

Cut a 7/8" square from cardstock. Sandwich between tape. Peel off one liner and press Silver coil to center, allowing the loops to extend out each side. Dip edges into UTEE. Sprinkle with Purple micro mix. Remove liner from back side and sprinkle area with UTEE. Repeat on all squares.

Thread an accent bead onto a 1" piece of wire and loop both ends. Connect the beaded links to the squares with pliers. Finish by adding jewelry clasp.

For earrings, create the basic coil following the instructions on the Diamond Dangle earrings. Cut two rectangles of cardstock 1 5/8" x 5/8" or desired size. Repeat the technique as in the bracelet. Finish by wrapping with wire and desired accent beads.

Earrings 5/8" x 1 5/8"
Bracelet square is 7/8" x 7/8"

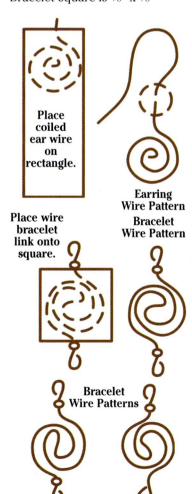

Place coiled ear wire on rectangle.

Earring Wire Pattern

Bracelet Wire Pattern

Place wire bracelet link onto square.

Bracelet Wire Patterns

Jewelry Fun

by Linda Peterson

Diamond Dangle Pendant & Earrings

MATERIALS: Olive Green cardstock • Redliner double-stick tape • *UTEE* (Bronze & Clear) • 20 gauge Brown *Artistic Wire* • Gold micro beads • Assorted bead mixes • Black fibers

HINTS: Always peel white liner off first.

CAUTION: UTEE becomes very hot and will burn fingers.

PENDANT INSTRUCTIONS: To make the coil curl, cut wire 7$\frac{1}{2}$" long. With pliers bend end into loop and continue forming a coil. Continue the coil until it is the size of a nickel. Bend wire upwards with pliers. Thread on beads. Create loop. Bend end down and twist around bottom of beads. Cut a 1$\frac{1}{4}$" Olive cardstock square. Sandwich the square between two layers of sticky tape. Peel red liner off one side. Place coil into position. Press coil down firmly with fingers. Dip edges of square into Bronze UTEE. Sprinkle on gold beads with fingers. Cover remainder with Clear UTEE. Hold square with pliers while heat setting UTEE. Peel backing off other side, sprinkle bronze UTEE over entire back and heat set.

Dangling beads: Cut 3 pieces of wire 2" long. Make a small loop in one end. Thread on beads. Finish opposite end with loop. Make 3 dangles. Make a jump ring from a $\frac{1}{2}$" piece of Brown wire. Bend until ends come together. Place beaded wires onto jump ring. Poke hole in bottom of pendant and insert jump ring. Cut 3 strands of fiber 36" or desired length. Thread wire through large bead to create a loop. Tie one end of the fibers to the loop. Tie a loop on the other side just large enough to hold the bead.

EARRINGS INSTRUCTIONS: Using the same technique as above, cut a 3" piece of wire. Coil as above to desired size to fit on $\frac{7}{8}$" squares. Bend coil upwards at a 90-degree angle. Add beads. Bend around to the back and trim to desired length to create fishhook. Cut out small $\frac{7}{8}$" squares. Press coil to front and finish using the instructions above.

Earring Wire Pattern

Pendant Coil Pattern

Earring Pattern

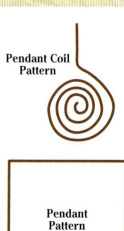

Pendant Pattern

Beaded Gifts

Beaded Gold Leaf Box
by Lizette LaForge

MATERIALS: Redliner double-stick tape (9" x 11" tape sheet; roll of 3/4" trim tape) • Gold micro beads • Multi-color bugle bead mix • 4 assorted jewels • Square metal box • 1 hank *Toner Plastics* Lace Nooodles • Lavender Ultra-fine glitter • Variegated Gold Leaf

INSTRUCTIONS: When you place tape on surfaces, be sure to remove any air bubbles before removing red liner by pressing with your fingers. Place tape sheet on the table, red liner side down, peel off the white liner and place the box top on the exposed tape. Turn this over and press tape firmly to box top removing any air bubbles. Trim tape to edge of box top. Remove red liner from box top. With plastic lacing, add designs to box top. Place jewels and bugle beads where indicated. Apply patches of variegated gold leaf. Dip box top into Gold beads, press down beads, pull off plastic lacing and set aside. Cover box bottom with 3/4" tape. Keep working fingers across red liner to keep as straight and smooth as possible. Trim overlapping tape at center back. Before removing red liner, use craft knife to trim away excess tape from edges of box. Remove red liner from box bottom. Create designs on box bottom with plastic lacing. Apply patches of variegated gold leaf. Dip into Gold beads, press the beads down and remove lacing. Sprinkle Lavender glitter all over box top and bottom, covering thoroughly. Shake off excess glitter.

TIP: Use a Ziploc bag and shake project with glitter in bag. Tap gently to remove excess glitter while project is still in bag.

Beaded Butterfly Plant Stakes
by Linda Peterson

MATERIALS: Redliner double-stick tape sheet • Micro beads in Clear and color of choice • *Artistic Wire* (18 & 20 gauge in coordinating colors to match beads) • 3/16" *Amaco* WireForm armature rod (stakes) • Assorted large glass beads • Various glitter colors • Hot glue • Clear acrylic sealer

INSTRUCTIONS: Working off the spool directly over the patterns with pliers, curl 20 gauge wire into patterns shown. Peel back white liner and place wire shapes on tape in position to create butterfly, placing top wing brace in place. Replace white liner and cut out butterfly. Remove white liner and dip into desired color of beads and glitter. Remove red liner and dip into clear beads.

For the body, string large beads onto an 8" piece of 18 gauge wire, with the largest bead at the top for the head. Finish the strand by coiling the wire or wrapping extra wire up through beads.

For the antennae, center a 6" piece of wire and wrap around head. Point each end up and curl ends with pliers. With 26 gauge wire 'sew' body onto wing area by poking through the tape and wrapping wire around beaded body. Shape wings as desired.

Attaching to stakes: Form an 18"-24" piece of 3/16" armature wire into a stand with a coil at the bottom. Thread 18" of 18 gauge wire through center of butterfly body, curling around beads to secure. Coil around a pencil several times and pull out. Wrap remaining wire around armature wire, stringing beads on wire as you coil around stake. When finished, spray beads with clear acrylic sealer to keep them from changing colors.

Designer note: These butterflies should be used as indoor decorative plant stakes only. The tape will not withstand the outdoor elements. Enlarge and reduce patterns to create different size butterflies. These butterflies can also be used as a decorative embellishment on wreaths and floral arrangements. Armature wire can be embellished by wrapping beads around the stem.

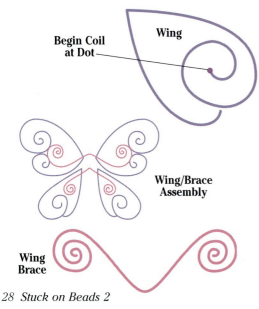

Top Wing

Begin Coil at Dot—

Wing

Wing/Brace Assembly

Wing Brace

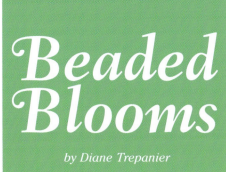

Beaded Blooms

by Diane Trepanier

Leaf Pattern

Flower Petal Patterns

1. Form petal shape with coiled wire. Apply Tacky tape to petal.

2. Apply seed bead mix to petal. Press beads firmly.

3. Coil ends of wire to form stamen. Tape together.

4. Place petals evenly around stem and bind with wire.

5. Wrap the end wires of leaves with floral tape and connect.

MATERIALS: *Artistic Wire* (1 spool each 22 and 26 gauge flower color; 1 spool each 22 and 26 gauge Green; 12" of 26 gauge Yellow; 1 spool of 28 gauge or smaller wire) • Redliner double-stick tape • Seed beads (assorted flower colors, Leaf Green) • Micro beads (Assorted flower colors, Green) • Ultra-fine glitter (Assorted flower colors, Green) • Wire coat hanger • Green floral tape • Wire coiling tool • Pliers (Chain-nose, Round-nose and nylon jaw) • Wire cutters • Scissors • Clear embossing ink • Small flat-bottomed bowl • Zip lock bags

Designer Note: These steps describe how to make the Red flower. Change petal and leaf shapes and sizes to create your own bouquet.

INSTRUCTIONS:

1. Using 26 gauge wire with the smallest dowel of the coiling tool, make three $1\frac{1}{8}$" and five pieces each $1\frac{3}{4}$", $2\frac{3}{8}$", $2\frac{5}{8}$" $3\frac{1}{8}$", and $3\frac{1}{2}$" in the flower colored coiled wire. Make one coiled piece $3\frac{3}{4}$" and four 4" pieces in Green wire.

2. Thread pieces of coil onto the 22 gauge wire. Cut the wire 3" longer than the piece of coil. Make a loop with each piece of coil and twist the 22 gauge ends together leaving long tails. To make the ends lie flat, press with nylon jaw pliers where the 22 gauge wire crosses.

3. Shape the loops into petal and leaf shapes with the end wires at the bottom of the shape.

4. Place petals and leaves on the sticky side of the Redliner tape; trim around edges. Make sure the tape is adhered well to the coiled wire. Note: Wipe a light coat of clear embossing ink on scissor blades (the inside and the angled edge) to prevent the tape from sticking to your scissors. Reapply the ink as necessary.

5. With seed bead mix in a small bowl, pour the bead mix over the sticky side of the Redliner tape (the release film should still be on the back side) for each petal. Press down on beads to make sure they adhere to the tape. Pour off excess beads, filling in gaps with a few beads. Repeat for all petals and leaves with appropriate color.

6. With micro beads in a small bowl, remove release film on the back of one petal. Place sticky side on the micro beads in bowl. Scoop up some micro beads and pour over the side with the seed beads to fill in gaps. Turn the flower over and rub micro beads in side. Shake off excess beads. Repeat for all petals and leaves with the appropriate color.

7. With flower colored glitter in a zip lock bag, place several flower petals in the bag, close tight, and shake well. The glitter will fill in the gaps to give the petals a solid look. Shake and brush off excess glitter. Repeat for all petals and leaves with appropriate color.

8. Cut the Yellow (stamen) wire into 4 pieces. With the tips of round-nose pliers, coil about three rounds at end of wire.

9. Cut 16" of coat hanger or heavy duty wire for the flower stem. Place a little Redliner tape around one end of the wire and place the stamen wires around the wire so that the coils extend $\frac{3}{8}$" upward. Bind the fine gauge wire to keep the stamens in place.

10. With the seed bead side facing out, bend the three small petals lengthwise over a pencil so they will cup into each other. Put a little tape around the end of the stem wire and place the center petals around the stamens and bind with wire.

11. Bend the wire tails of the next size petals at a 90-degree angle away from the seed bead side. With Redliner tape to hold the petals, evenly space them around the stem and bind with wire.

12. Bend the wire tails of the next larger size petals and place around the stem under and in the space between the previous petal. Bind with wire. Repeat with remaining layers using the next largest size each time and binding with wire. Wrap the stem with floral tape up to the last petals and back down.

13. Wrap the end wires of leaves with floral tape. Bend the leaves the same way as the petals. With the smallest leaf as the beginning leaf, bind two leaves opposite each other to the stem below the small leaf. Wrap with floral tape. Repeat with the last two leaves. Bend the completed leaf stem to the flower stem and wrap with floral tape. Cut the stem to the desired length.

Continued on page 30.

Beaded Blooms

by Diane Trepanier

Continued from page 29

Orange Lily Petal Pattern Cut 6

Beige and White Petal Pattern Cut 8

Beige and White Leaf Pattern Cut 2

Orange Lily Leaf Pattern Cut 2

Yellow Large Petal Pattern

Yellow Small Petal Pattern

Vibrant and lush, these beautiful creations will steal the show!

Yellow Flower Leaf Pattern

How-To Photos and Instructions for Beaded Blooms are on page 29.

Continued on page 32.

Gather your supplies and begin creating your fabulous beaded bouquet today!

Purple Flower Leaf Pattern Cut 2

Pink Flower Leaf Pattern Cut 1

Pink Flower Petal Pattern Cut 5

Purple Flower Petal Pattern Cut 6

Beaded Blooms

by Diane Trepanier

Tulip
Petal
Pattern
Cut 6

Tulip Leaf
Pattern
Cut 2

Gold &
Blue
Petal
Pattern
Cut 8

Gold &
Blue
Coil
Pattern

Gold &
Blue
Leaf
Pattern
Cut 2

How-To
Photos and
Instructions
for all
Beaded
Blooms
flowers
are on
page 29.